Superhero Superstars

Zoe Saldana

by Martha London

FOCUS READERS

BEACON

www.focusreaders.com

Focus Readers is distributed by North Star Editions:
sales@northstareditions.com | 888-417-0195

Produced for Focus Readers by Red Line Editorial.

Photographs ©: Sthanlee B. Mirador/Sipa USA/AP Images, cover, 1; Marvel Studios/Kobal/Shutterstock/Rex Features, 4, 29; Walt Disney Studios Motion Pictures/Photofest, 6, 22; Shutterstock Images, 8, 11, 13, 14, 18, 26; 20th Century Fox/Photofest, 16; Marvel Studios/Walt Disney Pictures/Album/Newscom, 20–21, 25

Library of Congress Cataloging-in-Publication Data
Names: London, Martha, author.
Title: Zoe Saldana / by Martha London.
Description: Lake Elmo, MN : Focus Readers, [2021] | Series: Superhero superstars | Includes index. | Audience: Grades: 4-6
Identifiers: LCCN 2020008136 (print) | LCCN 2020008137 (ebook) | ISBN 9781644933756 (hardcover) | ISBN 9781644934517 (paperback) | ISBN 9781644936030 (pdf) | ISBN 9781644935279 (ebook)
Subjects: LCSH: Saldana, Zoë, 1978---Juvenile literature. | Motion picture actors and actresses--United States--Biography--Juvenile literature. | African American motion picture actors and actresses--Biography--Juvenile literature. | Hispanic American motion picture actors and actresses--Biography--Juvenile literature.
Classification: LCC PN2287.S255 L66 2021 (print) | LCC PN2287.S255 (ebook) | DDC 791.4302/8092 [B]--dc23
LC record available at https://lccn.loc.gov/2020008136
LC ebook record available at https://lccn.loc.gov/2020008137

Printed in the United States of America
Mankato, MN
082020

About the Author

Martha London writes books for young readers full-time. When she isn't writing, she can be found hiking in the woods.

Table of Contents

Chapter 1

Green Alien

Cameras hang from the ceiling. The **director** starts the **scene**. Zoe Saldana begins running across the deck of a spaceship. She plays Gamora in *Guardians of the Galaxy*.

Gamora is a highly trained fighter. She's a master of martial arts.

Gamora first appeared in Marvel comics in 1975.

Laser shots hit the wall behind Gamora. Sparks fly. She sees guards at the end of the hall. She kicks the guns out of their hands. Gamora is trying to escape the enemy spaceship with her team.

After the scene is finished, Saldana takes a deep breath. Gamora is strong. Saldana works hard to play her. Acting is more than a job. Saldana loves bringing her characters to life.

Fun Fact

Saldana is bilingual. She speaks both English and Spanish.

CCI
+FILM
MA
CCI
LM

Chapter 2

Dancing

Zoe Saldana was born on June 19, 1978, in New Jersey. Her mother is from Puerto Rico. Her father was an **immigrant** from the Dominican Republic. Zoe spent her early childhood in the United States.

Saldana attends a party at the Los Angeles Contemporary Museum of Art in 2017.

Her family moved to the Dominican Republic when she was 10.

Zoe started taking dance lessons there. She joined a dance school. Zoe tried many types of dance. For example, she learned jazz and Latin-style dance. But ballet was her favorite.

Zoe's family moved back to the United States when she was 17.

Fun Fact

Zoe has two sisters, Mariel and Cisely.

Saldana was awarded a star on the Hollywood Walk of Fame in 2018.

She tried to keep dancing. But ballet was hurting her. So, she found a new way to express herself.

Zoe joined an acting group. It was called FACES. FACES performed plays that had positive messages for teens. Zoe loved performing. She began to work with other theater groups. For example, Zoe also performed with the New York Youth Theater. An **agent** saw her in one of the theater's plays. The agent was impressed by Zoe's talent. So, the agent helped her find **roles** on TV shows. It was the start of her career.

Saldana laughs with her costars for the movie *Missing Link* in 2019.

Chapter 3

Rise to Fame

Saldana acted in TV shows in the 1990s and early 2000s. Her first movie role was in a film about ballerinas competing for a lead role. Saldana was able to use her ballet skills for the movie.

Saldana smiles for cameras at the first showing of *Avengers: Endgame*.

Artists used computers to turn Saldana into a blue alien.

At first, Saldana mostly acted in supporting roles. Then she got a major part in 2009. She was cast as a lead character in a **science fiction** movie. She played a blue alien.

Saldana was excited to be in the film. She had loved science fiction as a child.

In 2014, Saldana was cast as Gamora in *Guardians of the Galaxy*. She got to play an alien again. However, acting in the two movies was very different.

Fun Fact

Saldana has been in several music videos. For example, she acted and danced in the video for "Free Me" by Sia.

Saldana went to the Cannes Film Festival in 2014. Cannes celebrates creative international film.

Saldana wore **motion-capture sensors** all over her face and body when she played the blue alien. To play Gamora, Saldana wore layers of makeup.

Both movies were very successful. They helped make Saldana a star. Saldana uses her fame to make a difference. For example, she works with FINCA. This group gives money to women. The women use the money to start businesses. They can support themselves with the money their businesses earn.

Fun Fact

Saldana runs a movie company with her sisters. They focus on sharing women's stories.

INSIDE HOLLYWOOD

A Specific Green

Artists had to decide what shade of green Gamora should be. First, they made a mold of Saldana's head and shoulders. They covered her in a green, slimy paste. The paste dried into a plastic mold. Artists used the mold to create a copy of Saldana's face. They tried different shades of green on this copy. Artists wanted the color to be bright. But they did not want audiences to be grossed out. Saldana did not have to sit through these color tests. But her makeup routine could take up to five hours to complete.

Gamora is a kind of alien called a Zen-Whoberi.

Chapter 4

Guarding the Galaxy

Saldana leads an active life. But she still had to work extra hard to get ready to play Gamora. For example, she learned martial arts because Gamora is a great fighter.

Gamora and the other Guardians prepare for battle.

Saldana wanted to make sure her acting was believable.

In a fight scene, things happen fast. The director wants to make sure every actor can be seen. Saldana learned the fight moves quickly. She used her dancing skills to help her. Learning fight

Fun Fact

Saldana did some of her own stunts. In one stunt, she jumped from a 30-foot (9.1-m) ledge.

***Guardians of the Galaxy* was one of the biggest moneymakers of 2014.**

moves was like learning the steps of a dance.

The *Guardians of the Galaxy* movie came out in 2014. No one was sure if it would be successful.

Saldana poses for cameras at the first showing of *Guardians of the Galaxy* in 2014.

The characters in the movie were not as well-known as most other superheroes. As a result, some people worried that fewer people would want to watch it. But the movie was a huge success. Its characters attracted many new fans.

In 2017, Saldana returned to play Gamora in a second Guardians of the Galaxy film. She also appeared in *Avengers: Infinity War* and *Avengers: Endgame*. Saldana looked forward to filming a third Guardians movie.

Saldana will continue to act. She loves playing different roles and bringing her characters to life.

FOCUS ON

Zoe Saldana

Write your answers on a separate piece of paper.

1. Write a paragraph summarizing the main ideas of Chapter 2.
2. Saldana enjoys science fiction. What kinds of movies would you want to act in?
3. In which performance did Saldana catch the attention of an agent?
   - **A.** a play with the New York Youth Theater
   - **B.** *Guardians of the Galaxy*
   - **C.** *Avengers: Endgame*
4. How might Saldana's dance training help her as an actor?
   - **A.** It helps her learn her lines.
   - **B.** It helps her play a more believable alien.
   - **C.** It helps her learn the steps in a fight scene.

5. What does **supporting** mean in this book?

At first, Saldana mostly acted in ***supporting*** *roles. Then she got a major part in 2009.*

A. most important
B. small or minor
C. encouraging

6. What does **cast** mean in this book?

She was ***cast*** *as a lead character in a science fiction movie. She played a blue alien.*

A. given a position in a dance group
B. offered a role in a movie
C. taught how to do ballet

Answer key on page 32.

Glossary

agent
A person who helps an actor find jobs.

director
A person who is in charge of making a movie.

immigrant
A person who moves to a new country.

motion-capture sensors
Electronic stickers that record the movements of an actor's body and send that information to a computer.

roles
The parts actors play in a television show or movie.

scene
A specific place and time during a movie or play.

science fiction
A type of story that often includes imagined future technologies and takes place in space.

stunts
Actions involving difficult skills or danger.

To Learn More

BOOKS

Bray, Adam. *Marvel Studios Character Encyclopedia*. New York: DK Publishing, 2019.

Delmar, Pete. *Zoe Saldana*. North Mankato, MN: Capstone Press, 2017.

Green, Sara. *Visual Effects*. Minneapolis: Bellwether Media, 2020.

NOTE TO EDUCATORS

Visit **www.focusreaders.com** to find lesson plans, activities, links, and other resources related to this title.

Index

Answer Key: 1. Answers will vary; **2.** Answers will vary; **3.** A; **4.** C; **5.** B; **6.** B